ANASHA - MERRY CHRISTMAS '91

LOVE,

GRAMPY + GRAMMY

Arctic Fives Arrive

Elinor J. Pinczes • Illustrated by Holly Berry

Houghton Mifflin Company
Boston 1996

For information about this and other Houghton Mifflin
trade and reference books and multimedia products,
visit The Bookstore at Houghton Mifflin on the World Wide
Web at http://www.hmco.com/trade/.

The text of this book is set in 14 point Clarendon.

Printed in the United States of America
WOZ 10 9 8 7 6 5 4 3 2 1

Library of Congress Cataloging-in-Publication Data

Pinczes, Elinor J.
Arctic fives arrive / Elinor Pinczes : illustrated by Holly Berry.
p. cm.
Summary: A counting book in which animals in groups
of five share a hilltop to view the northern lights.
ISBN 0-395-73577-7
[1. Counting. 2. Zoology — Arctic Regions — Fiction.
3. Auroras — Fiction. 4. Stories in rhyme.]
I. Berry, Holly, ill.   II. Title.
PZ8.3.P558676Ar 1996
[E]—dc2O 95-3693 CIP AC

For Dennise, our first arrival

— E.J.P.

For my little bear, Gwendolyn, with love

— H.B.

One late Arctic day, not too far from the bay,
five snowy owls gracefully flew.
They spotted a mound, the tallest around,
where small birds could have a nice view.

Deciding to light, the owls circled right,
while making one final survey.
It looked like a place with plenty of space
for the animals headed their way.

The five snowy owls, all fine-feathered fowls,
were peacefully taking their rest.
But hoots filled the air as up popped five bears
to join them atop the hillcrest.

Those bears were delighted but far too excited;
each owl hip-hopped out of harm's way.
The bears rubbed their jaws and licked icy paws;
once groomed, the bears planned to stay.

5 10 5 10 5

The owls wondered then if the rest would fit in.
Counting by fives, that's five, ten:
Five polar bears on pigeon-toed paws;
and five snowy owls with long, curvy claws.

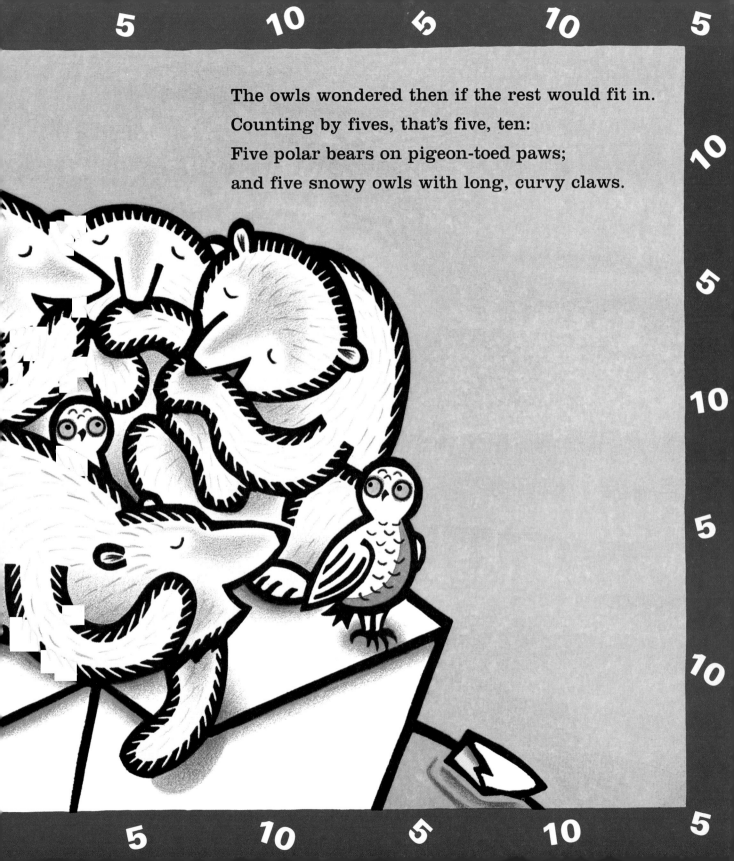

10

5

10

5

10

5 10 5 10 5

The bears settled down as the owls looked around
and spied ermine making the climb.
From ten occupants came a series of grunts,
when they shifted themselves one more time.

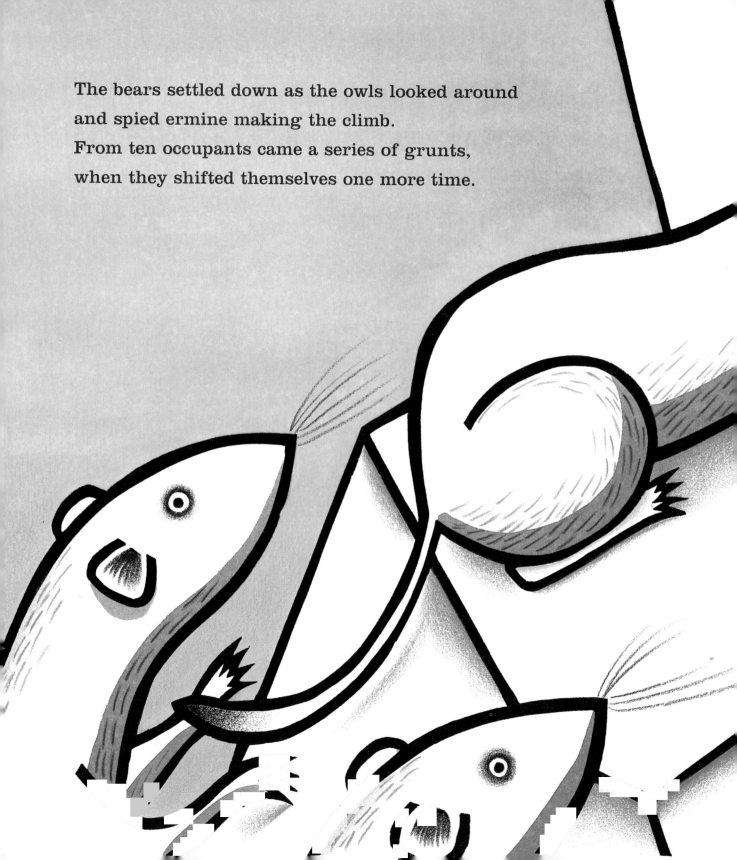

Tiny ears twitched and long whiskers switched
on the ermine surveying the view;
all anticipating, while contemplating
if others would climb the hill, too.

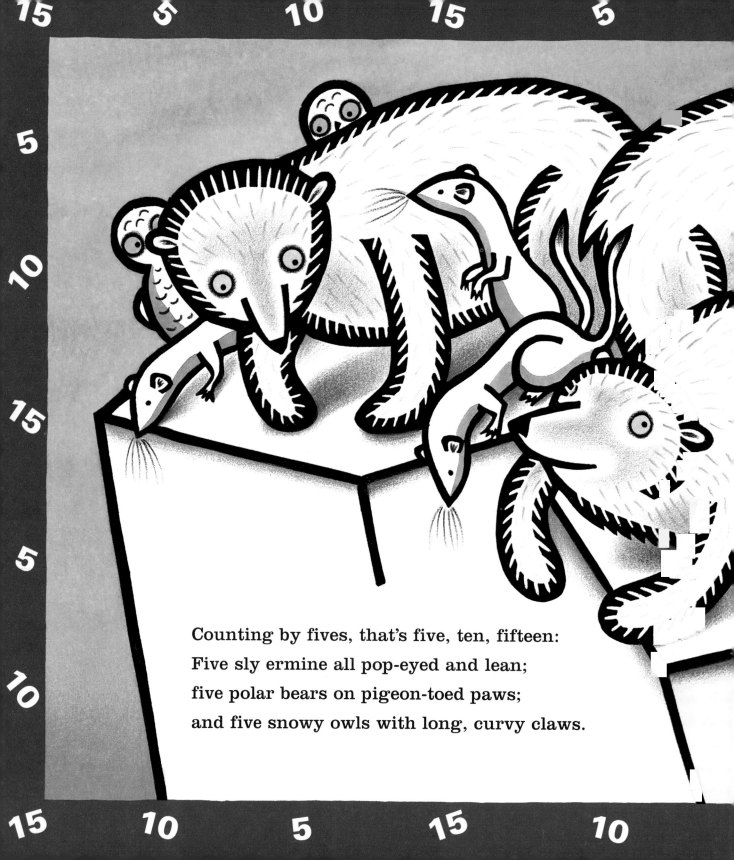

Counting by fives, that's five, ten, fifteen:
Five sly ermine all pop-eyed and lean;
five polar bears on pigeon-toed paws;
and five snowy owls with long, curvy claws.

Fifteen restless critters, all with the jitters,
felt something huge quaking the ground.
They heard walrus clapping, tail fins aflapping,
and knew who'd be next on the mound.

Each animal lifted, then suddenly shifted,
as fat walrus rumbled their way.
The five shut their eyes and heaved heavy sighs,
because of the weight pulled that day.

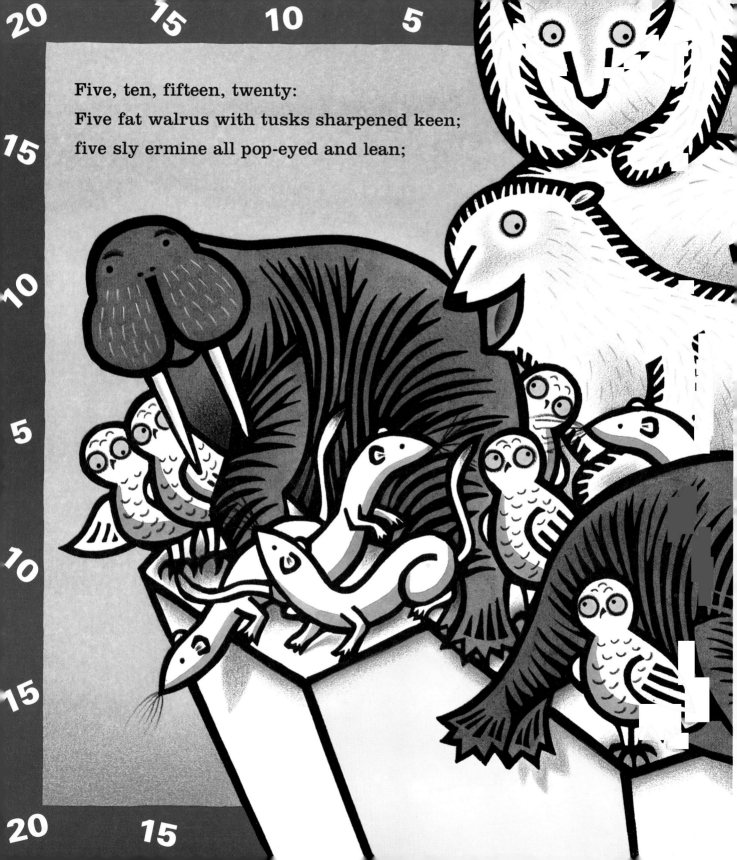

Five, ten, fifteen, twenty:
Five fat walrus with tusks sharpened keen;
five sly ermine all pop-eyed and lean;

five polar bears on pigeon-toed paws;
and five snowy owls with long, curvy claws.

Twenty animals now, all fitting somehow,
saw Arctic hares thump the packed snow.
They must move again, for the hares to fit in,
though there wasn't much space left to go.

The pert Arctic hares all wiggled their ears,
still numb from the chill of the day.
Pleased to be there, with time yet to spare,
the hares nimbly squeezed in to stay.

That's five, ten, fifteen, twenty, twenty-five:
Five Arctic hares whose ears dip and dive;
five fat walrus with tusks sharpened keen;
five sly ermine all pop-eyed and lean;
five polar bears on pigeon-toed paws;
and five snowy owls with long, curvy claws.

Suspense filled the air. Then out of nowhere
came musk oxen stumbling topside.
Twenty-five shuffled; to make room they scuffled,
for the new guys seemed overly wide.

The oxen looked beat. When they stamped their feet,
snow spattered the entire throng.
Once wedged into place, they stared into space
and hoped no one else came along.

That's five, ten, fifteen,
twenty, twenty-five, thirty:
Five musk oxen who timely arrive;
five Arctic hares whose ears dip and dive;

five fat walrus with tusks sharpened keen;
five sly ermine all pop-eyed and lean;
five polar bears on pigeon-toed paws;
and five snowy owls with long, curvy claws.

The white Arctic hares hip-hopped everywhere,
excited to get under way.
Each fat walrus clapped, all five ermine yapped,
and the polar bears started to sway.

Then sheer energy from electricity
was felt in the heart of each beast.
There were snowy owl *whos* and musk ox *moos*
as a rainbow of hues flickered east.

A soft, frosty glow slowly covered the snow,
while the bright colors lit the dim night.

They'd all come to see a great mystery —
the phenomenon called "Northern Lights."

Their order reversed, the watchers dispersed:
thirty, twenty-five, twenty, fifteen, ten, and five.
The small snowy owls, all satisfied fowls,
were last, since the first to arrive.

The owls flying high in a dark Arctic sky,
were pleased with their choice for the show.
Perhaps one day, at another display,
they would gather again in the snow.

DATE DUE

JAN 13 01	
MAR 7 02	
FEB 1 0 2004	
MAY 2 8 2004	
JUL 0 1 2004	
AUG 2 5 2005	
AUG 0 8 2006	
AUG 2 2 2006	